AF327193

HARLEY-DAVIDSON:
THE CUSTOMS OF
ARLEN NESS
30 Years of Hand-Crafted Motorcycles

by
Timothy Remus

First published in 1993 by Wolfgang Productions Inc., 19265 Orwell Av North, Marine, Minnesota, 55407, USA.

ISBN number: 0-9641358-0-9

Printed and bound in the USA

HARLEY-DAVIDSON:
THE CUSTOMS OF
ARLEN NESS
30 Years of Hand-Crafted Motorcycles

by

Timothy Remus

Acknowledgements

Now that this project is finally ready to be shipped to the printer, it's time to thank all the people who helped in various ways. At the top of the list are Arlen and Bev, as well as their son and daughter Cory and Sherri, for their help and encouragement.

The photographs in this book come from a variety of sources. Many are my own, though a significant number come from Arlen's archives. Most of the more recent studio-style shots credited to Arlen's archives were actually done by Carmina Besson, in-house photographer and the woman responsible for the very good looking Arlen Ness catalog. Some of the older archival film was not marked in any way and thus it's impossible to credit the photographer, though I'm indebted to each and every one.

Because this is my first book publishing project, there are some additional people to thank. Like my old friend Mike Urseth who helped me design the book and then did the computer layout. And another old friend, Steve Hendrickson, edited the manuscript and also did repair and scanning of the black and white photographs.

I am proud to say this book is just like Arlen's Motorcycles - born in the USA. This at a time when the common wisdom insists that all color printing must be done on the Pacific Rim. I wish to thank the crew from Riverside Color and PGI Incorporated, the separation house and printer respectively, for great work, competitive prices and for their willingness to go the extra mile so we could not only produce the book here, but do it on a very tight schedule.

Finally, I must thank my lovely and talented wife, Mary Lanz, for all the proof reading and more importantly, her moral support when I hit those inevitable low spots that come with any big project.

Introduction

Speaking of Introductions, I was introduced to Arlen Ness roughly five years ago as I prepared to collect the material necessary for the first book, Arlen Ness: Master Harley Customizer. Since that occasion I have enjoyed many pleasant hours, photographing Arlen's bikes and working with Arlen at the store or house. A person could have a worse job than mine, working with a man who is intelligent, easy going and very, very talented. Five years ago I described Arlen as a gentleman, I can only say that the ensuing five years have confirmed that first impression.

Work on this book started almost as soon as the other book was finished, at least in the sense that there seemed, from the beginning, that there would be the need for another book. To say that Arlen has produced new material since the first book was unveiled five years ago, is perhaps the understatement of the century. Not only has Arlen produced significant new designs, the whole world of custom Harley-Davidsons has gone on fast forward during the same time period.

While the first book put Arlen's history into one chapter and his bikes in the others, this text takes a different approach. There are five chapters here, and each chapter contains both biographical information on Arlen and information on the motorcycles.

The motorcycles are a reflection of the man who designs them, thus it seems appropriate to have biographical information included in the same chapter with bikes built during that part of Arlen's life.

In looking over the bikes, from the oldest to the newest, a few things about Arlen become obvious. First, Arlen has evolved, as do most artists, and learned something from each bike he built. Second, Arlen likes new ideas, no matter how radical they seem at the time they are built. In fact, some of his ideas that seemed pretty far-out at the time they were unveiled, have become standards of the custom bike field. Third, that though Arlen works hard at his trade, he truly has a talent for design, a gift for building motorcycles with lines and proportions that somehow look "right."

Rather than start this book where the other leaves off, I elected instead to start earlier - with anecdotes that precede anything in the other book - and run later with as much current information as I could cram into the book. So while there is some material common to both books, it has been kept to a minimum.

What you hold is a history of one man and his work. An attempt to describe in one relatively short book the work and workings of a very complex and creative man - Arlen Ness.

CAL
3K4899

Chapter One

Before Motorcycles

Arlen's first hot rods have four wheels

The California Kid

Arlen Ness grew up in the community of San Lorenzo, California, across the bay from San Francisco, and graduated from San Lorenzo high school in the spring of 1957. For the young Arlen Ness school was OK, he got good grades and always had plenty of friends. But like many of his classmates, what really fascinated this young man was cars and motorcycles.

Dad was strict, however, and explained that any cars Arlen bought would be purchased with his own money. By his fourteenth birthday Arlen was earning his own spending money setting pins at the local bowling alley after school and on weekends. After graduation Arlen worked for the Post Office as a mail carrier and later drove a delivery truck for his father's furniture business.

"No Motorcycles"

Though it seems hard to believe, Arlen Ness grew up without any motorcycles. It was Arlen's father who established the no-motorcycles rule, which meant that most of Arlen's early vehicles were cars instead of motorcycles. The one exception was a certain Cushman scooter Arlen brought home during his early high school years.

Arlen remembers the scooter and the constant repairs vividly, "I don't think I was ever off that scooter. I didn't have a permit yet, so I had to stay close to home. I rode it around the block hundreds and hundreds of times each day. I must have worn a groove in the concrete in front of the house I rode that scooter around so much. It had a body and a two-speed transmission. The sprocket on the transmission was keyed to the transmission output shaft, and I was always sheering that key. Of course we didn't have the right key, so we would cut a small washer in half with the hacksaw and use that for a key, until I shifted the scooter about six more times and then the key would shear again and the whole thing started over."

The Cushman was Arlen's first "motorcycle," though it would be a long time before he got to ride another. Before Arlen was old enough to get a permit and actually ride it on the street, Dad made him sell the beloved Cushman. Forbidden from buying another motorcycle, four-wheeled hot rods would occupy Arlen's free time during the rest of high school and well into his adult life.

Arlen's first car was a less-than-stellar hot rod, "it was something not-so-great like a '41 Plymouth four door," remembers Arlen. "I didn't have a license and it was just like the Cushman. I could drive it around the block but that was all. I'd load up every kid in our neighborhood, I think we got thirteen kids in there once, and then it was just like the scooter, we went around the block and around the block and around the block a million times."

Arlen's first "decent" car was a '51 Mercury which he promptly slammed to the ground and re-upholstered with a lot of help from his mother Elaine. The Mercury was followed by a '51 Caddy that Arlen drove to Tijuana for one of those Mexican custom upholstery jobs so popu-

One of the few good pictures of a young Arlen Ness shows him on an early chopper style bike (probably his first Knucklehead) complete with springer fork and no front brakes. Arlen Ness Archives

lar at the time. Arlen's next car was a little T-bucket that he towed home on the end of a log chain - because the T-bucket didn't have an engine.

Now, instead of just installing a flathead or a used V-8 from the junk yard Arlen came up with a better idea. Why not buy a real race engine and install that to create a true hot rod? True competition engines cost a lot more than most young men can afford, but as they say, "where there's a will, there's a way." Arlen didn't have any more money than the average young man, but he did have more drive and a certain cleverness. When Arlen saw a dual-engined dragster flip at the strip one Sunday, a light went on. The driver escaped unhurt, but one of the Cadillac engines was torn from the frame and rolled down the asphalt during the accident.

Arlen offered to buy the engine, complete with broken cast-iron bell housing and smashed valve covers. Now he had a full-house Caddy V-8 that everyone else thought was scrap. Except that Arlen found a fella who could weld the cast-iron by using special welding rods in his arc welder. Persistent and crafty, Arlen soon had the motor repaired and installed in the T-bucket.

Arlen remembers that T-bucket as "quite a ride." The T-bucket was also the first full Arlen Ness paint job. "I painted it orange with some paint I got for almost nothing from a friend of mine," remembers Arlen.

More than just a wild ride, the T-bucket was the first true Arlen Ness custom. Never mind the fact that it had four wheels instead of two. Arlen got the motor - one that most people considered too powerful for the chassis - inexpensively and then found a way to repair it. After adapting the drag race motor to the frame, he painted it and installed a new interior. The result was a true hot rod, built at a fraction of what anyone else would have spent - a nifty little T-bucket unlike any other on the street.

Family Man

The hot rod T-bucket didn't come along until five years after graduation, and by then there were plenty of other things going on in Arlen's life. During his senior year, Arlen met Bev Rego, a sophomore at a different school. After dating throughout the rest of her high school years, Arlen and Bev were married after graduation. There was just one problem, Bev didn't like motorcycles any more than Arlen's father and told Arlen in no uncertain terms that she, "wouldn't be married to anyone who rode a motorcycle."

So Arlen kept his projects confined to things like T-bucket roadsters, customized in the

---

I must have worn a groove in the concrete in front of the house I rode that scooter around so much.

---

evenings after working as a truck driver for his father's furniture business. In 1961, Sherri, Arlen and Bev's first child was born, and two years later their son Cory was born.

Two young children tend to keep a father at home. When Arlen could break away it was often to spend a few evening hours hangin' out on East Fourteenth street, the "Main Drag" of San Leandro and the other communities on the east side of San Francisco bay. Arlen would show up in his Cadillac and later the T-bucket, to show off his early paint jobs and to see what the rest of the boys were doing on the avenue.

East Fourteenth was a mixed bag of enthusiasts. There were hot rodders with souped up old coupes and drag racers with fast '55 Chevys. Setting in their own small groups were the bikers with a variety of hardware. Triumphs and BSAs from England, parked next to native-born

Harleys and Indians. Though he tended to hang with the car guys, the two-wheeled machines spoke to Arlen with their lean lines, sparkling chrome and loud pipes.

Today, Arlen remembers that, "In those days I didn't really know one bike from another, I just knew what I liked - the long lean looks of some of those bikes, that's what appealed to me."

The Die is Cast

The bike that appealed to him the most was an old Harley-Davidson Knucklehead, and in 1966 Arlen bought the bike for $300 and then asked a friend to ride it home - because the only two wheeler Arlen had ever ridden was the Cushman scooter.

Once the new bike was home, Arlen had his work cut out for him. First, he had to placate his young wife Bev, the one who hated motor-cycles. Second, he really wanted to paint the Knucklehead. Finally, he had to learn how to ride a motorcycle.

When all three tasks were complete, Arlen showed up in his old haunts on East Fourteenth with the new Knucklehead. Judged by his peers, the bike was a shining success. Successful enough that Arlen was soon painting gas tanks and motorcycle parts for other riders in his small home shop.

Almost two years after buying the Knucklehead, Arlen stripped it down, added new accessories and applied a new, wilder paint job. His friends were mighty impressed with the newly re-created Knucklehead and encouraged Arlen to enter it in the Oakland Roadster show. Arlen took their advice and came home on Sunday night with a first place trophy.

That was Arlen's first show and first trophy,

but certainly not his last. The shows helped to focus more attention on Arlen and guide more people to his small home painting shop.

Arlen's home shop eventually got so busy that there didn't seem to be enough hours in the day to get all the work done. The small shop was often busy from the time Arlen got home until well past a normal bedtime. Bev remem-bers the late nights and the hassle of trying to run a normal family, "I would finally just have to go into the garage and announce that it was time for dinner. Not that I meant to be rude, it

---

The bike that appealed to him the most was an old Harley-Davidson Knucklehead, and in 1966 Arlen bought the bike for $300 and then asked a friend to ride it home…

---

was just that there were so many people there all the time and sometimes it seemed like they would never leave."

Arlen came up with a solution of course, like he always does. The solution involved more work and more risk but also more opportunity. If Arlen could just do enough work to justify a small store, then the store would draw people away from the house and allow Arlen to expand the business.

THE MOTORCYCLES

Arlen's first bikes exhibit styling cues from the period, including such standard items as

Following pages: Not just any old Knucklehead, this one displaces 100 ci, force-fed by a Magnuson blower. Note the elaborate engraving. Belt drive consists of a double-wide drive pulley at the crankshaft and a driven pulley of the same size mounted to the blower.

SAN LEANDRO
ARLEN NESS

4.25/85 V 18
M45
MICHELIN

angular tanks and springer forks. They also exhibit a flair missing from other of their peers. A certain continuity in the design that was often missing from those early choppers. Of note also is the fact that Arlen's bikes were always a little different from the others. For one thing, Arlen always built "runners," or bikes that actually worked when they hit the pavement. Arlen's bikes also carried a certain design integrity missing from other bikes. Even early Arlen Ness bikes have a certain "flow," or sense that all the parts fit together to create a great motorcycle design and not just a collection of bright shiny parts.

Untouchable

Arlen's First motorcycle, the one he bought

Arlen wanted more than just a big stroker motor. He wanted something that made tons of power, looked great and also made a statement about Arlen Ness.

---

with money won in a semi-professional bowling league, has been built and rebuilt over the years. As Arlen explained, "In those early days I didn't have enough money to buy a new bike each time, so sometimes I would just re-build a bike into a whole new machine."

In its current incarnation, Untouchable represents a very sophisticated package from another era. A bike with style and class, a winning design with a variety of innovations that show

Arlen Ness to be a very clever bike builder -then and now.

The front fork, for example, might look like just another springer from those bygone days. If you look closely, though, you notice that the fork has been reinforced on both sides with small diameter tubing and that instead of using conventional brake hoses, Arlen ran the the brake fluid through that tubing to each front brake caliper. The dual disc front brakes are an innovation of their own. Arlen was among the first to insist on installing front brakes, at a time when builders were stripping the bikes of all those "unnecessary" accessories. It's important to remember that part of what separated Arlen from other early builders was the fact that his bikes were always built to run - and to stop.

The frame for Untouchable is a classic collaboration between Arlen Ness and master builder Jim Davis. Crafted from small diameter chrome-moly tubing, the long hardtail frame is a graceful piece, with curves and arches in place of straight tubes wherever possible. Like the front fork, the frame tubes are used to route oil from the hidden oil tank to the engine.

The oil tank itself is incorporated into the large rocket shaped gas tank. Built mostly from flat sheets of steel with dimples on the bottom to clear the Knuckles, the tank is the work of Bob Monroe. It's interesting to note that Arlen continues to work with Bob Monroe, and that he worked with Jim Davis until Jim's death in a motorcycle accident in 1989.

Under the long gas tank is a 100 ci Knucklehead with a stroker crank and oversize pistons. Arlen wanted more than just a big stro-

19 79 CAL
BK4899

ker motor. He wanted something that made tons of power, looked great and also made a statement about Arlen Ness. The answer turned out to be a Magnuson blower tucked neatly up under the front of the tank, plumbed to two Weber sidedraft carbs that hang out front and center between the fork and the frame. All those cubic inches would be a bear to kick start, so Arlen installed electric start. Well, he really didn't just install an electric starter. Actually he installed a whole Sportster transmission and obtained the electric start that way.

Drive from the engine to the transmission is by toothed primary belt, partially enclosed by a custom housing. Another belt drives the blower off the left side at a ratio of one-to-one. Built before the advent of belt drive to the rear wheel, a chain carries the power to the spoked rear wheel, though it seems odd to have a Big Twin with the chain on the right side of the bike instead of the left (Sportsters drive on the right, Big Twins on the left).

Early Shovelhead bike is built around an even earlier Harley-Davidson VL frame with single downtube. The bike looks simple and stubby by today's standards.

The red paint is Arlen's own, with gold leaf by Jeff McCann. Dick DeBenedicties painted the gangsters on the tank, to lock in the Untouchable - Elliot Ness - theme borrowed from the old TV show. The sheen has dimmed over the years, the plating on the engine is elaborate and done mostly with gold or silver. Jeweler Dave Murray started by engraving silver plate, then inlaid the plate with gold before riveting the plates to the rocker boxes.

Taken all together, Untouchable is quite a piece of work. Though Arlen may not be the first to run oil through the frame or to bolt a blower to a Knucklehead, he is the first to combine all those clever mechanical elements in such a good looking package. More than just an old chopper or nostalgia bike, Untouchable is a bike ahead of its time - Arlen's first really wild piece and an indicator that there would be plenty more where this one came from.

Life on a Hardtail was made somewhat more reasonable by the hinged and suspended riders seat.

Rear fender is supported by frame and small sissy bar. Note the unusual foot pegs and shifter location.

Arlen has built hundreds of motorcycles and over the years, most of those have gotten away from him. In the early days he often had to sell one to build another. Even later when money was less of a problem persistent fans would sometimes talk Arlen into selling a bike after it was a year or two old.

Older Arlen Ness bikes have become very collectible with a price tag double or triple what a similar bike, built by someone else, might bring. This makes it tough for Arlen to buy back many of his old bikes. They are coveted by collectors and expensive to boot. There have been a few times, however, when Arlen could buy back an old piece of his personal history, usually in need of a complete restoration.

The Yellow Shovel is one such bike, built during Arlen's very early years and sold a long time ago. That's the bad news, the good news is the fact that the bike's owner brought it by the shop recently for Arlen to see - and Arlen was able to purchase the bike.

As delivered, the bike was in poor condition and suffered the ravages of too much time spent in a damp garage. The paint was bubbled and gone, replaced by surface rust. But everything was there, mostly unaltered from the day, twenty some years earlier, that it left Arlen's shop.

Arlen started the restoration by pulling the motor out of the frame so everything could be painted. The frame is an old Harley-Davidson single-bar VL unit, dating to the 1930s, prized in those early chopper days for its simplicity and style. These frames were so popular that when the supply of stock frames finally dried up, Arlen began selling an improved version -

Winged apparition on the Sportster tank is a Horst creation. Shovelhead engine has been "freshened" since Arlen bought the bike back and was almost ready to run at the time of this photo.

the first complete Arlen Ness frame. Bolted to the front of this particular VL frame is the skinny springer fork, made by modifying a stock Harley-Davidson fork (remember this was in the days before Arlen or anyone else made springer fork assemblies).

The Shovelhead engine is one that Arlen bought new for the bike when it was built. When the bike came back, the old Shovelhead was in need if some TLC. Arlen pulled the motor part way down, so some of the covers could go out for new chrome plate. Before being reassembled, the heads were treated to a valve job to ensure it would run as well as it did twenty years earlier.

At the time this bike was built, there was only one gas tank to have and that was a Sportster tank. Behind the tank is a single seat and a small pillion for a presumably small passenger. The Hardtail frame design made it easy to support the rear fender with a simple, chrome-plated sissy bar.

"In those early days I didn't have enough money to buy a new bike each time, so sometimes I would just re-build a bike into a whole new machine."

In fact, the whole bike is pretty simple and spare, in the style of the day. This particular example differed from others by having more detail than the bikes parked next to it at the curb or show. The rims for example measure 21 and 16 inches for the front and back, just like they all did, though these are chrome plated. Both are shod with period-correct Avon tires. Like the rims, the engine and transmission cases sparkle with chrome plating.

Arlen did the original paint in yellow lacquer before sending the bike over to Horst, one of California's best known painters, for some of his wonderful graphic work. When it came time

---

But when the new store is finished there will be a large area designated as museum space. And then more people will be able to see not just how it is, but how it was.

---

to repaint the bike, Arlen had the frame sand-blasted and the tank sanded before applying multiple coats of the same yellow paint, only

this time in a urethane base. Then he called Horst, who agreed to do another detail job just like the one he did all those years ago.

The bike currently resides in Arlen's too-small upstairs museum, open only to special guests. But when the new store is finished there will be a large area designated as museum space. And then more people will be able to see not just how it is, but how it was.

In the late 1960s, there was only one fork to have, and that was a springer - preferably a very narrow and very shiny one.

The old Sportster features a pair of those famous Ramhorn handle bars and a very bright paint job.

Chapter Two

Arlen Takes The Plunge

The first store

The Dream

Arlen's evolving skill as a painter brought more and more people to his small shop at home. While most of those people were customers, they made it hard to maintain anything like a regular family life. A seed was planted in Arlen's brain and soon he shared it with Bev: what if they opened a small store? He could still do the work at home, but the customers would come to the store, not the house. Arlen could continue to paint, and maybe they could sell some additional accessories at the store.

Though it took some time to convince Bev, she and Arlen eventually went shopping for a small storefront in the only logical area - East Fourteenth Street. "A hundred dollars a month was a lot of money to us then," recalls Bev, "we were both pretty nervous when we signed that lease. And of course Arlen still had to keep his regular job because we knew he didn't have enough motorcycle business to pay all our bills."

The store itself was tiny, meaning that Arlen still did all the paint work at home. Because he had to hold down the regular job, the store didn't open until 6:00 P.M., unless Arlen's brother Kevin came down and opened the store when he got out of school. Closing came whenever Arlen could get everyone out of the store.

During this period Arlen bent up a new set of handlebars for one of his personal projects. The "Ramhorn" bars attracted a tremendous amount of attention on the street and soon Arlen found a shop that could bend them in quantity and another to do the chrome plating. The new bars were Arlen's first big commercial success. People came from all over to buy a set of those bars and Arlen remembers how good it felt whenever he went down to open the store in the evening, "People were lined up outside the door, waiting to buy a pair of those bars, it was really great."

The Ramhorn bars showed Arlen to be more than just a motorcycle painter - more than just another guy with customized Harleys in the local shows. Though many of his designs have been "ripped off" over the years, the bars were the first of many innovative Arlen Ness designs and an indication that he could make a living from more than just his paint jobs.

After two years of running the store in the evenings and hauling furniture during the day, Arlen was ready for both less and more. Less pressure balancing the two jobs and more time dedicated to the expanding motorcycle business.

Bev kept the books for the growing business, Arlen asked her what she thought. Could they make enough money from the business alone to live on? When Bev gave her opinion that, yes, they could make enough from Arlen's fledgling motorcycle business, he gave notice at the day job and posted the new hours at the store.

On a Roll

The decision to work full time at the business was the start of some heady growth for Arlen and Bev. The original storefront measured only about 200 square feet. About the time Arlen went full time with the business, the photo studio next to the store moved and Arlen

It wasn't much by today's standards - measuring only 200 square feet - but the little hole-in-the-wall store on East Fourteenth Street was a start for the young painter named Arlen Ness.

was able to rent an additional four hundred square feet of space. Suddenly they had three times the space and almost double the monthly rent.

Those additional square feet were filled with more parts and accessories, both Arlen's and those from outside manufacturers. The Ramhorn bars were the first big success, but Arlen soon added front frame sections, complete frames and a variety of sheet metal parts. Though Arlen would soon offer a variety of gas tank designs, the first custom tank was a simple, mostly round design, fabricated by Bev's father, a sheet metal man.

Hydraulic forks fell from favor and Springers became the fork of choice. Stock and modified springers just weren't narrow enough

The exhaust driven blower is fed fuel and air from a single Weber carburetor. Sportster engine uses low compression pistons and four special camshafts designed specifically for force-fed engines.

The left side of Arlen's Lowliner hot rod shows off the unusual open primary, the wrap around oil tank and the single exhaust pipe.

for Arlen, who soon began manufacturing his own line of ultra-narrow springer forks which the magazines soon termed, as the "Ness springer."

As the business grew at Arlen's Motorcycle Ness-Ecities, so did the hassles of finding reliable shops to manufacture the parts. Arlen decided to open a machine shop and fabrication center of his own. The facility that he opened was a partnership between he and Bev, and one other person. With a reliable supply of quality parts and a growing name recognition, Arlen figured the time was ripe to open more retail outlets. Soon they opened another two stores, one in San Mateo and one in San Jose. Each

Long and lean, this bike borrows lines seen at the drag strip - even to the point of using a slick on the rear. Extreme narrowness is interrupted only by the license plate bracket and the turbocharger.

store was owned in partnership agreements similar to the fabrication center.

The Arlen Ness Look

At about this same time Arlen met Larry Kumferman, editor of Custom Bike magazine. Larry was the first magazine editor to "discover" the interesting and innovative bike builder from San Leandro, California. While most bike builders were going to longer and longer forks and front frame sections that went uphill to the neck, Arlen began building bikes long and low with top frame rails horizontal to the ground and springer forks of modest extension. On top of these frames sat diamond or rocket-shaped tanks manufactured in Arlen's own facility.

Sportsters became the bike of choice for Arlen Ness and many of his peers during the 1970s. Arlen's bikes from this period continued the long low theme first seen in magazine fea-

Boomerang tanks were seen on only a few of Arlen's early bikes. These were fabricated by Bob Monroe and feature gold leaf work by Jeff McCann. Drag bars mount to short risers.

ture bikes of about 1973. Springer forks with no front fender, small bobbed rear fenders, angular gas tank shapes (which were easy for

Stock and modified springers just weren't narrow enough for Arlen, who soon began manufacturing his own line of ultra-narrow springer forks which the magazines soon termed the "Ness springer."

men without any metal bending equipment to fabricate) and hopped-up engines were the order of the day. These were minimalist bikes, bikes with a look all their own.

Magazine coverage brought more interest in the bikes, and in the parts used on the bikes. Letters from all over the country began to arrive, most wanting to know, "How much for one of those cool diamond tanks," or for "a pair of those chrome rear struts?"

The first Arlen Ness catalog was nothing more than a typed sheet with a listing for each part and the price. The price sheets were sent to anyone who mailed in a request. Jeff McCann, well known painter, is the one who finally sat down with Arlen a few years after he opened the store, and helped him design and lay out a real catalog with photos and product descriptions.

Arlen's business had grown tremendously in only a few years time, from a small home shop

Instead of the more common 21 inch spoked wheels and no brakes, this Lowliner uses 18 inch Morris wheels with dual disc brakes. Note the gold plated lower fork legs and elaborate engraving.

36

to a real store with three satellite operations. Arlen and Bev were experiencing the headaches of running a business. The toughest part proved to be the outside stores and the fabrication center. Arguments and disagreements with the other partners became a major distraction, so two years after opening the other facilities Arlen bought out each store and brought the parts and tooling into his store on East Fourteenth.

With the outside manufacturing facility closed, Arlen was often faced with a dilemma whenever he considered manufacturing a new part. In some cases, Arlen would manufacture the part himself. Self manufacture meant Arlen

Rear brakes feature two aftermarket calipers mounted to a single bracket and connected to a common master cylinder.

and Bev had to come up with the cost of set up and tooling before manufacture could begin. In order to avoid the cost of tooling, Arlen sometimes tried licensing arrangements.

Though the idea sounds good on paper, the concept never actually worked very well for Arlen. Sometimes the license fees never got paid. More often the designs were copied and manufactured in Taiwan, all without Arlen's permission or knowledge.

Despite the setbacks and growing pains, the Arlen Ness store on East Fourteenth Street did grow. After ten years time, the six hundred square feet of space was jammed right to the rafters with tires, tanks and various parts. What had seemed so palatial only a few years earlier suddenly seemed no bigger than an overstuffed closet at home. Arlen and Bev went looking at storefronts again, until they found a spot just up the street, still on East Fourteenth, with more than twice the floor space of the first store.

THE MOTORCYCLES

Sportsters were the order of the day and Arlen built his share in both hard and soft-tail versions. From relatively simple bikes Arlen gravitated to more elaborate designs with blowers or turbochargers. By the middle and late

Left side of Mail Call is very mechanical with the belt drive and shaft used to deliver power to the blower. Note the heavy use of both gold and chrome plate - and the engraving. Arlen Ness Archives

Mail Call started life as a stock Sportster - before Arlen added a new front frame section, rear Super Struts and blower. Nearly all the items could be ordered from Arlen's catalog. Arlen Ness Archives

1970s Arlen was building a number of serious bikes each year and getting good coverage in magazines like *Street Chopper* and *Custom Bike.*

A turbocharged Low Rider

Though the meanings have changed, the term Low Rider was used by magazine writers of the mid-1970s to describe a long, low Arlen Ness style Sportster. The turbocharged model seen here, with the elaborate body and paint work, might be called the best of that breed.

The bike's foundation is one of Arlen's Lowliner frames with a six inch stretch and 40 degree fork angle. Instead of the more typical springer fork and spoked wheels, the bike uses a

The small Magnuson blower tucks up tight against the engine's right side. Ignition is by magneto and all the engine covers are gold plated and engraved. Arlen Ness Archives

hydraulic fork and 18 inch Morris wheels on both the front and the back. Bolted to each wheel are the drilled disc brake rotors, with two in front, an innovation at the time. Each front rotor is gripped by one engraved caliper, while the rear rotor is clamped by two small calipers.

The engine is what we would call an Ironhead Sportster - though at the time this bike was built no one had heard of an Evo. In order to ensure that this Sporty had enough snort, Arlen bolted on a turbocharger, a popular power boosting option at the time of this bike's construction. The Turbocharger is fed by a Weber side-draft carburetor and provides plenty

Mail Call has the right look for the time with a springer fork, 40 degree fork angle, 21 inch front wheel and minimal accessories. Arlen Ness Archives

of visual pizazz on the bike's right side. The turbo also means that there is only one exhaust pipe - on the left side instead of the right.

Though most of Arlen's Sportsters used simple rocket or diamond-shaped tanks, this one features a pair of "boomerang" tanks. Fabricated by Bob Monroe from flat steel plate, they run along the top tube and then turn down to follow the frame's lower legs. Seen on only a few of Arlen's bikes, these tanks tend to merge with the frame and provide more surface for elaborate paint schemes.

Engraving was very popular when this Sportster was built, in fact Arlen offered the ser-

Rear fender is - you guessed it - a catalog item dressed out with gold leaf designs from Jeff McCann. Note the gold plate, vestigal chain guard, chrome plated Super Struts. Arlen Ness Archives

vice directly through the shop. The intricate designs on this bike are the work of Rudy Pena and can be seen on most of the engine covers as well as the lower fork legs.

Rounding out the equipment list is a wrap-around oil bag built by Bob Monroe and drag style handle bars mounted to short risers. The rectangular master cylinder for the rear brakes mounts to the unique, open primary, all on the left side, because this bike shifts on the right. The paint on this bike is a deep maroon applied by Arlen with gold leaf work by Jeff McCann. The seat is a little solo number covered in matching velvet.

This best-of-breed is also one of the last to survive. An endangered species if you will, an example of a style called by the press "uniquely Arlen's." Once as common as the VW "bug" this turbocharged model is one of the last to be seen rolling across the wilds of California.

Mail Call

Arlen is no stranger to the Oakland Roadster Show, having displayed at least one new bike every year since taking Untouchable to his first show. In 1979 Arlen's new bike was known as "Mail Call." The unusual name was Arlen's idea, meant to help illustrate the fact that nearly all the parts used on the bike could be ordered through the catalog.

The bike built to help promote the catalog side of the business hardly looks like a mail-order project, and that's the whole idea. The frame started as a stock Harley-Davidson item before Arlen cut off the neck and added a new

Next pages: This Arlen Ness built Sportster was recently brought back to life after being buried for 16 years in an old garage. Jeff Hackett

Mail Call was displayed with two tanks in order to illustrate the wide range of options available to a

potential catalog buyer/builder.   Arlen Ness Archives

front section - known on the street as a hard-head - intended to stretch the bike out and keep it nice and low. Bike builders were still enamored with the hardtail look and Arlen's answer is a bit more elegant than most. Instead of replacing the shocks with simple struts, Arlen built this pseudo-hardtail with a pair of his Super Struts, made from quarter inch steel plate and designed to tuck behind the frame so they would blend with the horizontal fender struts.

Arlen designed the bike with two different gas tanks, each one with a nearly identical paint job. If you wanted the Sportster look, there was the cut-down Sportster tank with flat bottom. Or, if the long rectangular look was more your style, you could have the long rocket tank that stretched from the neck all the way to the seat. The balance of the sheet metal consisted of a "taillight" rear fender constructed of hand-laid fiberglass and an aftermarket light assembly.

Arlen obviously wanted this to be a bike that anyone could build, yet he needed to make it his very own. Thus, there are some special little touches: like the 24 carat Midas touch on the rims, engine covers, and fork springs. Even the magneto body, pushrod tubes and complete swingarm are gold plated.

And if that wasn't enough, Arlen built more than just a standard Sportster engine. On the right side is the Magnuson blower, mounted up close to the cylinders and breathing through a Weber carburetor. The drive belt and pulley are on the other side, with a shaft running across the front of the engine driving the blower through a ninety-degree adapter. Instead of gold, the blower and drive are either chrome

S&S carburetor feeds an enlarged 1000 cc Sportster engine with magneto ignition, straight pipes and lots of chrome plating. Only minor work was needed to resuscitate the engine after it's long sleep. Jeff Hackett

plated or painted to match the bike. The cylinders are minus the lowest fins, while the rest of the fins are chrome plated and "hexed."

The red paint was applied by the master himself, while the gold leaf is the work of Jeff McCann. And yes, at the time the bike was built, complete paint jobs with pinstripe and gold leaf work could be had - all through the mail.

Mail Call looked great sitting in Arlen's display area at the Roadster show and succeeded in proving that a Sportster like this could be built almost entirely from catalog parts - though in over fifteen years no one has ever seen another one quite like this one.

Garage Sale Special

Bill Haar of Seaside, California is an old fan

The old Sportster is a reminder too that Arlen wasn't born designing Ferrari bikes, but rather developed his considerable talents one bike at time.

---

of Arlen Ness. during a recent search for an old Arlen Ness frame he discovered what might be called the deal of a lifetime.

"I went into Arlen's Shop," explains Bill, "and asked if anyone knew where I could find an old frame or front section for a Sportster project I had at home. Leonard told me about a guy who he thought had a frame, or maybe a whole bike that could be stripped to sell the frame. I called the guy and then went up to his house. When he opened the garage door, there was this chopper from the early '70s. It was all there, but it hadn't run since about 1977. There were leaves piled underneath it and spider webs all over."

Bill was able to show his new pride and joy to Arlen during Sturgis week. When Arlen saw the bike he told Bill that yes, he did most of the work on the bike, but that it actually belonged to a friend of his.

The bike is certainly period-correct for the early '70s. The Sportster frame is minus the rear shocks and carries one of Arlen's front frame sections. The springer fork is long and lean, and supports a 21 inch front tire. There are no front brakes and only a drum brake in the rear. Mounted on top of the frame is one of Arlen's diamond gas tanks. The colorful paint job on the long tank and bobbed rear fender is by none other than Horst.

The old Ironhead engine has been souped up, but only mildly. First, there's the displacement increase to 1000 cc with larger barrels and pistons. Then the breathing was enhanced with larger ports and valves. The carburetor is an

Unlike the turbocharged Lowrider bike, this "Rip-Van-Winkle" machine uses a long Arlen Ness springer and 21 inch front tire. Front brakes were often seen as an unnecessary accessory. Jeff Hackett.

early S&S while the ignition is by magneto. Externally the engine relies on chrome plated rocker boxes and covers for plenty of sparkle, contrasting with barrels painted flat black.

Incredible as it sounds, not only was the bike all there, but all it needed was air in the tires and gas in the tank before it ran. Then Bill had to do a lot of clean up work - but that was all. The paint and chrome seen on the bike today is the same paint and chrome that was on the bike when Bill first saw it in the garage.

What Bill brought home from that garage is not just an old motorcycle, but a piece of history. A part of the past for both Arlen Ness and all of us who enjoy motorcycles. The old Sportster is a reminder too that Arlen wasn't born designing Ferrari bikes, but rather developed his considerable talents one bike at time.

Though it was actually built for one of his friends, this bike carries an Arlen Ness front frame section, *springer fork and one of Arlen's diamond tanks with great paint by Horst. Jeff Hackett*

HARLEY-DAVIDSON
PRIMO BELT DRIVES

Chapter Three

Making a Statement

Arlen builds a really wild one

Business is Good

There was a down turn in the custom bike building business during the early and mid-1980s. Instead of building wild custom bikes, many riders simply bought the already "customized" Wide Glides or Low Riders from the factory. Some bikers simply kept their old ride because there wasn't enough money to buy or build a new one.

It was at about this time that Arlen and Bev

moved into their second store, and it was hard for anyone hanging around that new shop to tell that times were bad. With more floor space Arlen was able to stock more parts, both other people's and his own. And with a small shop at the store he was able to do more work on customer bikes. Though everything seemed to be rolling along just fine, Arlen thought it was time to build a really radical bike. Something that would be more than just another custom motorcycle, a bike so outrageous that it would really make a statement about Arlen Ness and his abilities.

Two Bad combined two Sportster engines in one frame, fed fuel by two Dell' Orto carburetors and a belt-driven Magnuson supercharger. Arlen built it with center-hub steering like a car, and fuel and oil tanks integrated into the frame and 'body" of the bike. Magazines hailed Two Bad as "an astounding study in fine design, engineering and craftsmanship." It's hard to get depressed about the state of business when your new twin-engined motorcycle has just won the solid silver trophy awarded at the Harley-Davidson Show in Daytona Beach, Florida.

Though some small "chopper shops" were

experiencing hard times, Arlen was running at full throttle. In addition to Two Bad, Arlen cranked out a series of new custom bikes in the early and mid-1980s. Sportsters fell from favor and suddenly everyone wanted a Big Twin. Bikers wanted to build Knuckles, Pans and Shovelheads, and Arlen was right there with new Big Twin-powered bikes and parts.

Strictly Business, one of Arlen's new bikes from the period, featured a 100 ci Shovelhead engine and four-speed transmission, set in a new frame. Hardtails became passe, displaced in part by Arlen's new swingarm frame, designed for clean lines and a low seat height. When Harley-Davidson brought out the five speed transmis-

Building Two Bad posed many problems, with plumbing near the top. Bob Monroe solved the exhaust riddle by creating this tubular sculpture on the right side.

Arlen and Bev pose with Arlen's newest, wildest, double-engined creation, circa 1979. Arlen Ness Archives

sion, Arlen collaborated with master frame builder Jim Davis, and another new frame made its way into the Arlen Ness catalog. In addition to new frames, Arlen added new cafe fender designs and even a small cafe fairing to the catalog listings.

What started more than ten years before as a simple price list evolved into a full blown catalog with four-color cover and hundreds of listings. Many of the items were Arlen's own, available only through the Arlen Ness catalog. Thus growth came not only from the new, larger store, but also from increasing catalog sales.

Shortly after moving into the second store, a new kid started hanging around in the afternoons. Just another part-time employee, neater than most and always polite. He came in after school and helped in the shipping department. Quiet and thoughtful, this new kid seemed to take on more and more responsibility as time went by. Finally, people began to ask Arlen, "Who is that new kid I see in here all the time?" "That's my son Cory," answered Arlen.

More Shows

At his core, Arlen Ness is a designer, always creating. Strictly Business, Orange Blossom and Blown Shovel came out during the time Arlen and Bev were at their second store. All went to shows, but unlike Arlen's earlier bikes, they were not placed in competition. Arlen realized that it was, in his words, "unfair" to be competing with his customers and stopped placing his bikes in competition for trophies and awards. His bikes continued to appear however, usually at the insistence of the show promoters.

Not only did the promoters want the bikes, they wanted Arlen too. This quiet man from San Leandro, California became something of a star in his own right. Show promoters wanted him to come along with the bikes, and manufacturers began to seek him out for product endorsements. No one seemed more surprised

with this turn of events than Arlen.

In addition to designing bikes, there were contracts to design parts for other companies in the aftermarket. These companies figured that if you wanted your parts to fit and look just right, who better to design them than Arlen Ness.

Though the new store was big enough for a small shop, Arlen continued to do most of his work at the home shop. With a mill, lathe and small paint facility, Arlen still found it easier to work here instead of the store. Without customers or ringing telephones, Arlen could work well into the wee hours trying new ideas: How best to make a fender fit just right, or how to get the best impact from a new color scheme for a hand-fabricated gas tank.

By the middle of the 1980s the new store wasn't big enough anymore, so Arlen and Bev doubled the floor space again by moving part of the operation into the adjacent building. Fiscally conservative, they continued to expand the business, but in a slow, controlled fashion.

THE MOTORCYCLES

By the time Arlen moved into the second store, the custom motorcycle world was going through a series of changes. Cubic inches became king and suddenly everyone wanted a Big Twin. Pushed by this move to Big Twins and his own expanding talents, Arlen built a series of new bikes unlike anything built before.

Two Bad

It's hard to describe a bike as well known and elaborately praised as Two Bad. Two Bad might simply be described as one hell of a motorcycle and one hell of an accomplishment for the man who built it.

Twin-engined bikes had been built before of course, but never like this. Arlen's creation features two Sportster engines, one transmission, one blower, two carburetors, four tanks for oil and gas and one center-hub steering mechanism, all set into a long chrome moly frame.

Arlen started with two 900 cc Sportster motors equipped with 1000 cc cylinders and pistons. After eliminating the transmission and generator from the front motor, Arlen set the two engines together on the shop floor and discussed the situation with Jim Davis. "I want to bolt these two engines together," explained Arlen, "and set them in a frame that will keep the profile real low. It will have to be a long wheelbase, but then if I get the front wheel way out ahead of the engines a regular fork won't work."

Building Two Bad would create more than one "insurmountable" problem, and solving one problem always seemed to create another and another.

The long low profile that Arlen wanted was accomplished with the Jim Davis frame incorporating torsion bar suspension and center-hub steering (like that used on a car, built for Arlen by Don Engle). Arlen didn't want any gas tank on top of the engines, so the tanks were incorporated into the frame and body of the bike. If there wasn't any gas tank on top, then they didn't need any top frame tube - a great concept, though it left the frame pretty weak, requiring the engines to become stressed members.

Once Arlen had solved most of the insurmountable problems and built a rolling chassis, there were still a number of challenging mechanical riddles to solve. Like how to connect the motors, how to drive the blower, where to mount the carburetors and a dozen more.

Let's see, one belt drives the blower while another connects the two engines and a third serves as primary drive to the transmission.

The blower is fed by a pair of Weber carburetors. Gas "tanks" can be seen above the carb, looking like part of the bike's body.

Because Arlen planned to mount the blower ahead of the front engine, it was logical to drive the blower from that same engine. A double-wide pulley bolted to the front engine's crankshaft allows it to drive the blower through one belt and be connected to the rear engine through another. The rear engine uses a similar double pulley on the crankshaft, with one pulley connected to the front engine and the other serving as the primary drive to the transmission. The design combines the power of two engines and passes it through to the transmission of the rear engine. From the transmission power is transmitted to the rear wheel by a conventional

Following pages: Larger than life, Arlen's creation sits on a display stand in the center of the store. Note the center-hub steering, torsion bar front suspension.

Without a top tube, engines must be bolted together to serve as stressed members. Each engine has its own magneto though they share fuel and air from the Magnuson blower.

chain on the bike's right side.

With the two engines bolted and belted together there was still the plumbing problem. How to get all that gas and air from the carburetors to the blower, from the blower to the engines and finally out the exhaust. The answer to the problem turned out to be Bob Monroe, who crafted both the intake and the "basket of snakes" exhaust system.

Because the blower was mounted so low the Weber sidedraft carburetors almost drag the ground, which looks pretty neat but created another of those little problems. Like how to get the gas to run uphill, from the carburetor to the intake valves, during the starting mode. The answer turned out to be a mini-fuel injection circuit fed by an electric fuel pump and used

Antique riders speeding across the rectangular gas tank add a nice touch to Arlen's new/old motorcycle.

Designed to look old, Nesstique is based on a special frame of small-diameter chrome moly tubing with *an extra long springer fork.*

only for starting.

Making gas run uphill wasn't the only thing that kept Arlen from starting the twin-engined beast. With no way to uncouple the two engines, cranking them over fast enough to start was another problem. Arlen tried golf cart batteries and bigger starters before settling for one beefed up Sportster starter and two batteries hidden under the body work.

After all the problems were solved and the bike was a proven runner, Arlen pulled it apart again for final molding and paint. The engines were completely disassembled and detailed. The barrels got chrome plating while the cases and rockers got gold plate instead. Arlen applied the purple paint and then asked Jeff McCann to apply some of his lovely gold leaf work.

It's not too hard to believe that Two Bad took two years to complete. The bike was designed to make a statement about Arlen Ness, and it succeeded like a million mega watt neon billboard. Every magazine both here and in

The engine for Nesstique is a mostly stock Ironhead Sportster mill. Oil tank is built into the gas tank.

Frame tubes are used to route oil to and from the tank.

62

Europe praised the bike and the bike's builder. Show promoters stood in line with requests for the bike. And when a skeptical onlooker at a show made a sneering remark about how the bike probably didn't run, Arlen started it by remote control from across the auditorium.

With the completion of Two Bad, no one would ever again doubt the abilities of a certain young bike builder named Arlen Ness.

Nesstique

Nesstique is Arlen's old/new Sportster based motorcycle, though it certainly shouldn't be dismissed as just another custom Sportster. Arlen wanted a bike with the look of a genuine

Rear wheel measures 21 inches in diameter and helps give that tall skinny look Arlen was after.

antique and the dependability of a modern motorcycle. A classic he could ride every day.

Antique bikes are tall and skinny, with small engines and rectangular gas tanks. Thus Arlen conceived a little sleight of hand to shrink the engine. By making the frame larger than necessary the engine became "smaller." The fork is a relatively long and very skinny springer, mated to special tiller-style handle bars. The tall skinny look is accentuated with the tall 21 inch tires mounted to slim, spoked rims.

Like most of Arlen's bikes, this one has some of those little special touches. The oil tank for

example is built into the Jim Davis frame and uses the front down tubes for oil lines. The engine has been sanitized with hexed (or made externally hexagonal instead of round) and chrome plated cylinders and gold plated rocker covers and magneto body. The magneto itself means this bike starts with a kick - batteries not required. Which helps to keep that old time, and very open, look that Arlen was after.

For the gas tank, Arlen took some pictures of old bikes over to the talented Bob Monroe. Bob built a rectangular tank from scratch and sent it back to Arlen's for molding. For paint

Arlen's Panhead carries a mostly stock engine in a rigid frame. Carburetor is an early S&S. Gas tanks are three- and-a-half gallon Fat Bobs.

Fishtail pipes and a wrap-around oil tank from Bob Monroe are all part of the styling cues for this special

Panhead. Note the disc brake rotor, tombstone tail-light.

66

Arlen chose a simple black paint job and a not-so-simple mural that makes the whole bike come together. George Waters did the mural across the top panel of the gas tank, an image of two early riders speeding across the countryside on their classic motorcycles.

Nesstique made the cover of at least one contemporary motorcycle magazine and went on to please thousands of people at numerous shows. Of all the bikes Arlen has built, Nesstique is most often remembered. Different from his other custom bikes, Nesstique is instead a classic, showing Arlen's wide ranging talents and his knack for building people pleasing motorcycles.

The Pan

Arlen Ness is a big believer in that old adage, "variety is the spice of life." Having already built Sportsters as hardtails, Softails and antiques, Arlen opted for something different - very different. Big Twins were becoming more popular and Arlen wanted to try out some new ideas.

As Arlen rolled the ideas for the new bike around in his head, he decided it should be powered by a Panhead engine. For styling he chose a look totally different from his own earlier work. Different in fact than what anyone else had done up to that time. The look is actually something Arlen borrowed from a certain early bike manufacturer named Indian. So while most of the world was still throwing away their fenders, Arlen was building a bike with fenders big enough to cover most of the wheel.

Arlen bolted the Panhead and four-speed transmission into one of his own hardtail frames and connected the two with a Primo belt drive.

On the front of the frame he hung a narrow Ness springer fork and 19 inch wheel with a Carlisle tire, while in back he chose a traditional 16 inch rim and Avon rubber. Dual discs from Hurst were used on the front while another disc, this one from Brembo, was used at the rear.

The Indian-style fenders are the work of Bob Monroe, formed to lay close to the tire with a small flip at the back of each one. The gas tanks are Fat Bobs from Arlen's catalog equipped with the traditional speedo and dash. A small clearance light rests on the top of the front fender while a tombstone taillight is mounted in back.

Like most of Arlen's bikes, The Pan was well received by the press and the crowds at shows and events. With a Big Twin for power and plenty of body work, this motorcycle helped to point Arlen Ness in a new direction.

Blown Shovel

Arlen Ness is a prolific creator of custom Harley-Davidsons. After nearly thirty years, there exist hundreds of bikes bearing the unique Arlen Ness stamp. And among this elite group of motorcycles, there are a few special bikes. Not just the larger-than-life bikes such as Two Bad, but bikes where everything turned out just perfect - where all the parts and paint come together with a certain very special harmony.

Blown Shovel is one such bike, built by combining a much-modified Arlen Ness swingarm frame with a supercharged Shovelhead. Rather than just build a hairy street bike with an enormous motor, Arlen created a bike with both power and grace, a bike that works whether its standing still or running down the highway.

Arlen started the project by contracting Carl at Carl's Speed Shop to build a better than average engine. "Mr. Go-Fast" had the boys in the shop assemble a special 80 ci engine using low-compression pistons designed for a blown engine, mated to stock connecting rods and flywheels. Carl did his usual five-angle valve job and a little port work at the same time. To operate the valves an Andrew camshaft was chosen, one with plenty of valve lift but minimal valve overlap, due to the supercharged engine.

The Magnuson blower is mounted on the right side, driven from the other side through a ninety degree adapter and shaft. Another belt, this one from Primo, connects the crankshaft with the four-speed transmission. The primary belt is contained in a special one-off polished housing crafted by Bob Monroe.

To give the engine plenty of visual pizazz, Arlen had a series of recesses milled into the upper housings and air snorkels for the twin S.U. carburetors, and in the rocker boxes as well. After the parts had been to the chrome plating shop, the recesses were painted with the same deep brown paint as the rest of the bike.

The blower too is a series of deep brown recessed areas contrasting with the polished ribs.

When it was all done, Arlen set this detail monster, this Big-Bad-Wolf of a Shovelhead into a very interesting frame. The frame is made up of an Arlen Ness swingarm chassis with a large diameter oval tube in place of the top tube. The oval tubing is the work of Steve Ellington, who took the round section steel tubing and placed it in an enormous press to create the oval look Arlen needed. The long oval top tube replaces the gas tank and gives the bike a lean, drag race profile. Arlen and Jim Davis built the frame with a six inch stretch and a 40 degree fork angle, to further exaggerate the bike's length.

At the front of the frame, a narrow fork of oriental descent mounts in custom triple trees. The rim and dual disc brakes also come from that same donor motorcycle. At the rear, Arlen

The rear brakes combine two, two-piston calipers (with milled surfaces), on a single bracket operated *by a common master cylinder.*

needed a really fat tire and found one in a 19 inch dirt track racing tire. Finding the correct rim that would mount to the Shovelhead proved somewhat more difficult, and finally a 19 inch front rim was split in two, widened and then mated to a solid center section and standard hub. The polished rotor bolts to the right side of the rear rim, squeezed by a pair of calipers, milled, polished and painted to match the pattern used on the engine.

Minimalist might best describe the body work used on this bike. Yet, this bike with no gas tank and only a vestigal rear fender relies on the minimal body pieces for much of its visual

Power for the blower originates on the left side at the crankshaft, then goes by belt to the shaft ,which in turn runs across the front of the motor to drive the blower through a 90-degree adapter.

impact. In front, the small fender mounted close to the tire and the cafe fairing combine to reinforce the bike's hot rod flavor. Instead of using a fairing straight from the catalog, Arlen asked Bob Monroe to fabricate small louvered panels from aluminum for each side. While they were at it, Arlen and Bob designed and built side covers to enclose the oil tank, and skirts that partly enclose the rear wheel. The final piece of Bob Monroe crafted aluminum is the small air dam, the one that hides the oil cooler.

The polished aluminum panels combined with the great Jeff McCann gold leaf work tend to mellow the full-race thrust of this Arlen Ness bike, providing another dimension to the appeal. More than just a hot rod or drag strip bike, this Blown Shovel is both elegant and awesome at the same time. A bike where all the pieces fit together to work and look better than almost any other.

Blown Shovel uses a very special Ness frame with an oval tube serving as both gas tank and frame member. Note the small air dam, unique primary cover and extensive use of aluminum covers.

Chapter Four

Hard Work Pays Off

Success on a larger scale

Fruits of his labor

When the decade of the 1980s drew to a close, Arlen Ness had already been customizing motorcycles for more than twenty years. During those twenty years, Arlen and Bev had seen the store and the business grow slowly and steadily, from a tiny store with 200 square feet to one with over 3000 square feet, from a one-page price list to a real catalog. Twenty years of consistently great designs combined with a tremen-dous amount of plain old hard work, meant that Arlen was positioned for success on a scale he never before imagined.

The new decade would bring with it more growth at a much faster rate. The expanding market for Harley-Davidson parts both here and in Europe, the popularity of customizing and the improving economy, all would work to put Arlen Ness at the top of the customized Harley-Davidson business.

Store Number Three

In early 1988 Arlen and Cory went looking at storefronts again. This time it wasn't a little 200 square foot hole in the wall, but rather a relatively large facility with room for a large retail store, offices, a shop, warehouse and even room to expand into the building next door. Though it was bigger, the new location was still in San Leandro and it was still on East Fourteenth Street.

As purchased, the new buildings needed some work. Instead of borrowing a lot of money for a complete renovation, Arlen hired a local contractor and biker to do the heavy work. Cleanup, cosmetics and paint were done by Arlen and Bev, with help from Cory, daughter

Sherri and some good friends. When they opened the store and warehouse, the facility measured about 5000 square feet. Next door was another building that came along with the deal, rented to someone else until Arlen needed the space.

The 1990s might be called the decade of the American Motorcycle. Though at one time only six hours away from a filing for bankruptcy, Harley-Davidson recovered to become the darling of bikers and non-bikers all over the world. By the early 1990s, motorcycle riders both young and old were lining up at their local dealer to buy a new Harley-Davidson.

Many of the buyers were new to the fold,

Cory's FXR is the work of a young designer with his own ideas. Big Wheels are his own one-off designs mounted to this very long FXR.

enticed by the growing acceptance of motorcycles and the mechanical integrity of the new Harleys. Suddenly it wasn't just okay to ride a Harley, it was really cool to ride a Harley-Davidson, preferably one with plenty of neat accessories and a wild paint job. For many people, those cool accessories could come from only one source - Arlen Ness.

New Outlets for Arlen Ness Parts

And for the first time, many of those Arlen Ness parts were available from more than just one source. No longer did fans need to call Arlen for a catalog. Now those cool Stealth mirrors and FXR side covers were available through the Drag Specialties catalog. Drag Specialties, an old established supplier of aftermarket Harley-Davidson parts, was the first large company to sign and honor an agreement to license and sell Arlen Ness parts. Given all the less than

Arlen and Cory's current store is not what you would call small (this is about half of it), but will soon be replaced by a bigger facility with more room for both products and complete motorcycles.

ME
METZELER

honorable relationships of Arlen's earlier years, he remains very pleased with the Drag Specialties relationship, "Fred and Jeff Fox, the two men behind Drag's recent success, are always very fair and honest in their dealings with me."

By this time Cory was playing a key role, having moved up from the shipping department years earlier. With a good head for business, Cory became very involved in the company's growth and began orchestrating much of the expansion. In addition to the relationship with

---

Arlen understands that he can't just build two or three nice machines per year, that sometimes he needs to do something so outrageous it really gets people's attention.

Drag Specialties, Arlen and Cory began to make inroads into the expanding European market. Arlen Ness dealers were established in Europe and Japan, providing customizers all over the world with a direct link to Arlen Ness parts. What started as a trickle of overseas business now accounts for nearly thirty percent of Arlen's sales.

The Arlen Ness Book

As the final measure of Arlen's credibility as the King of the Customizers, Motorbooks International, publishers of everything from Ferrari books to Model A manuals, chose to do a book on Arlen Ness. As Arlen tells it, "The book is very different from a magazine article, it really means something to people when they read about you in a book."

Product Endorsements

In the old days Arlen would sometimes do an endorsement for a carburetor or a chain, but it was usually a freebee. For Arlen those early endorsements were just another chance to keep his name in front of the riders. Now, companies like Metzeler tire were finally willing to do more than just give away a few tires in order to have the endorsement of Arlen Ness. But like his motorcycles, Arlen always made sure the products work - before he let anyone use his name.

The time spent in store number three has been very good to Arlen, both in terms of the business and in terms of the new bikes to roll out the door. Among the multitude of very successful new motorcycles there is one real stunner. One so wild it could only have come from Arlen Ness.

THE MOTORCYCLES

Most of us are familiar with the bikes in this chapter. They've been displayed on the cover of various magazines or ridden through the streets of Sturgis and Daytona. These newer bikes are either very modern, or very "old." While some leap into the future, others can only be called retro-designs based on bikes built twenty or more years ago. What they all have in common is a certain flair that distinguishes Arlen's machines from all the rest.

The Ferrari Bike

Ten years is a long time, and it was roughly ten years between the introduction of Two Bad and Arlen's next major piece, the Ferrari Bike. Arlen understands that he can't just build two or three nice machines per year, that sometimes he needs to do something so outrageous it really gets people's attention.

Arlen wanted a fully bodied bike, something elaborate and complex with beautiful flowing

80

lines. Planning and construction of such a bike would require talents outside his normal pool of subcontractors. Arlen often goes straight from the idea in his head, to the actual machine in metal, using only the simplest of sketches to convey his ideas to men like Bob Monroe who do most of the fabrication. This new bike Arlen had in his head was so complex that he hired Thom Taylor, an automotive artist better known for street rod work, to create the renderings of the bike - to take the ideas from Arlen's head and put them on paper.

When Arlen went to Thom Taylor, he already had a pretty good idea of the new bike's dimensions and overall look. Arlen and Jim Davis had already designed and built a rolling chassis, longer and wider than most, and powered by a very unusual V-twin.

Part of Arlen's Concept Collection, the Ferrari bike wraps an enormous V-twin in a some very stunning aluminum body work.

Another in the long evolutionary ladder, this FXR based Luxury Liner looks great in purple flames laid over black with wild flamed bags.

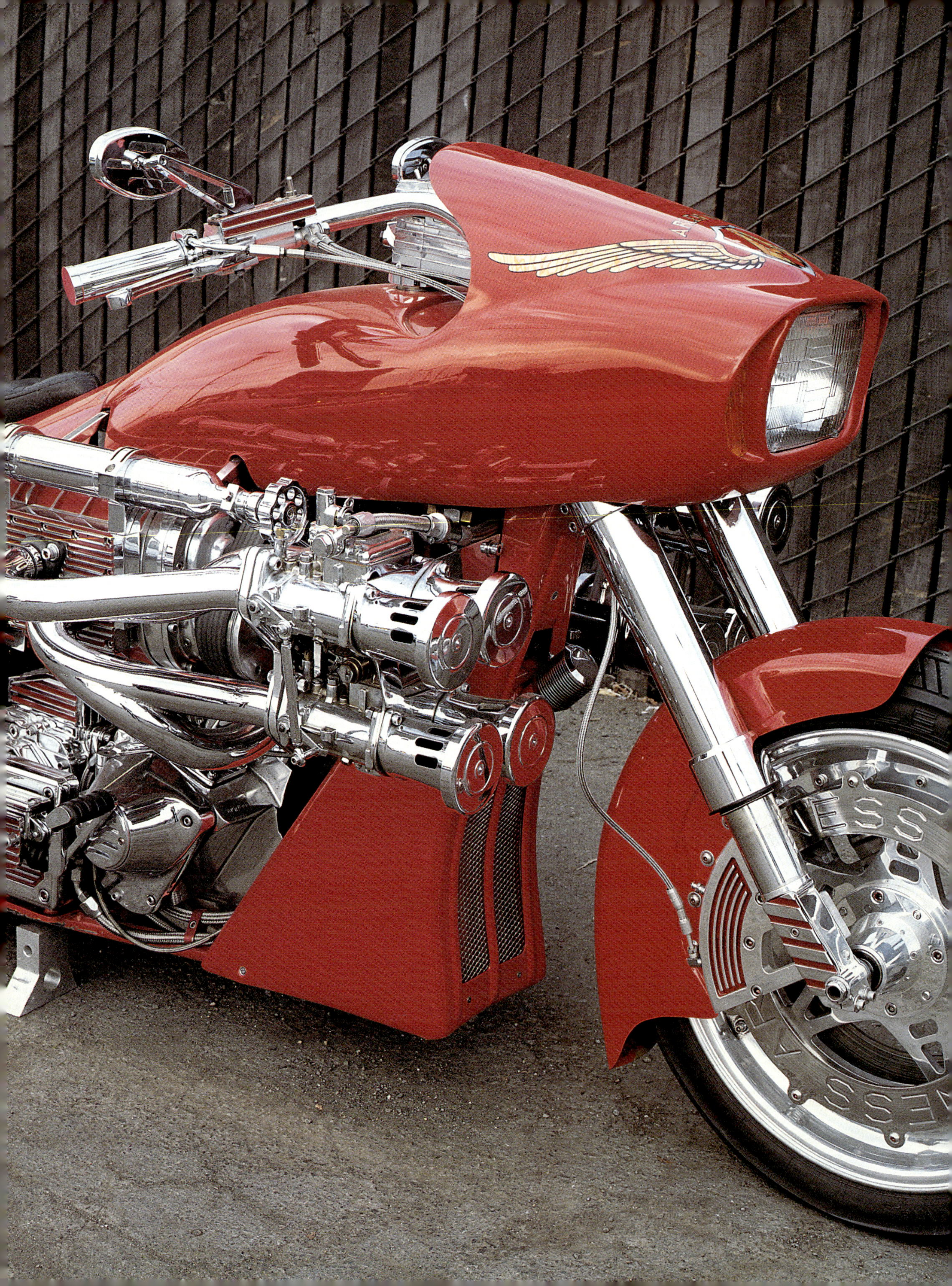

Arlen and Jim decided that the new fully
bodied bike would be a Hardtail, in order to
avoid the hassles of providing room under the
body for tire movement or worries about scrap-
ing the body work on the street as the bike went
down a bumpy street. Arlen insisted that the
frame be wide enough to accommodate a huge
rear tire, a 265/60-16 inch tire, wider than anything used on two wheels, except maybe a full-
on drag bike.

The frame that Jim built is a simple
Hardtail design, with two down-tubes running
from the neck, down and under the engine and
then running back to the rear axle. The top of
the frame is a single backbone that runs from
the neck to the seat area, where two smaller
diameter tubes connect and run back to the rear
axle on either side. The top backbone is reinforced with a smaller tube underneath, and the
area under the engine and transmission has
been "X-ed" but the frame is really quite simple.
Simply long enough for the bodywork, wide
enough for the massive rear tire and strong
enough to handle the torque of a 128 ci John
Harman engine.

Arlen wanted more than just a stroker
motor, he wanted massive torque in a very
dependable package. Racers say it's hard to beat
cubic inches, thus Arlen chose the Harman
engine, (designed by the late John Harman)
consisting of special lower cases, cylinders and
heads. The cases are designed to combine
Harley-Davidson flywheel assemblies with 4-

*The Dell'Orto carburetors mount to custom chrome
plated tubing all bent and fabricated by master craftsman Bob Monroe.*

1/4 inch pistons designed for a big-block Chevy V-8. The heads maintain that bigger-is-better-attitude with 2-1/8 inch intake valves and ports to match.

Once the engine was installed in the frame, Arlen sent the whole works down to Boyd Coddington's shop in Los Angeles, California.

Best known for his street rod work, Boyd assigned his best metal man, Craig Naff, to build from scratch the body panels for Arlen's new motorcycle.

Craig started by building cardboard templates to illustrate in two dimensions what the body and proportions would look like. With

The Golden Gate bridge is right there behind Arlen, you just can't see it because the fog rolled in at the

last minute - which just goes to show how hard it is to plan a photo shoot.

Arlen's approval and input, Craig went ahead and formed the body panels from aluminum sheet. In three months Craig formed panels so nice that they didn't need any body filler. So perfect that Arlen was to ride the bike in raw aluminum for some time, before he got around to painting it in brilliant House of Kolor red.

Once the body panels were finished, it was time to complete the mechanical aspect of this very one-off motorcycle. For a front fork Arlen chose a Simons upside-down design, mounted to the bike with special triple clamps machined by Darrell Hayes. Darrell went on to fabricate some very unique wheel and brake components for this very special motorcycle. The front calipers hold four pistons each, help to support the fender and squeeze fabricated rotors that bolt to the rim, not the hub. The wheel itself, made up of spokes shaped in an Arlen Ness "A" are also of Darrell's manufacture.

The rear wheel and brakes are similar to those on the front, with Darrell's four-piston calipers mounted inboard, between the drive sprockets (there's one on each side) and the wheel hub. The hub itself and the spoked center section are both Darrell's, bolted to the wide, two-part racing rim.

The rear wheel is driven by a pair of belts, one on each side, that run forward to the smaller drive sprockets. These sprockets are part of a jack shaft, connected through a short chain to the five-speed transmission. Finally, a Primo primary belt connects the transmission to the King Kong V-twin.

Arlen thought the Harman engine was a good start on the proper motor for the new bike. Cubic inches are good, but the bike needed more - more power and more sex appeal.

It's hard to beat the visual impact of a blower, and if one is good two must be better. How about if each blower is fed by two Dell'Orto carburetors. If that's not enough, let's mount a nitrous bottle and hardware on each of the Magnuson blowers. Then, the final touch, lots of chrome plating for the tubing, blowers and nitrous bottles. The blowers are driven by a single belt that gets its power from a 90-degree adapter that bolts to the primary cover on the

---

Among the best remembered bikes are the choppers, with hardtail frames, Panhead engines and springer forks.

---

left side. The whole affair, from the drive pulley to the driven pulleys for the blowers, is more of Darrell Hayes' work.

Finished in the reddest red you've ever seen and dripping mechanical detail from every pore, the Ferrari bike is another major winner from Arlen Ness. When push comes to shove, no one does it like the lad from San Leandro.

Flamed Pan

Just because Arlen was busy building ultra modern motorcycles like the fully bodied Ferrari bike or a new definition of what a Sportster should look like, didn't mean he didn't remember how Harley-Davidsons used to look. If Arlen's bikes could take us forward into the future, there's no reason they can't take us back into the past as well.

Arlen's flamed machine is for travelling, through time as well as space. The bike follows a certain formula dictated by the way things were and way we remember them as being. Among the best remembered bikes are the choppers, with hardtail frames, Panhead engines and springer forks.

Arlen's personal interpretation of this old theme started life as an aftermarket Hardtail frame. On the front of that frame Arlen hung a new springer fork from Paughco. Not a long

"ten over" springer, but a short stubby springer like they ran on the very first choppers. The handlebars - tall, ape-hanger bars of course - bolt directly to the fork legs. On the other end of the fork Arlen mounted a spoked, 21 inch rim without even a vestige of a front fender.

The rear rim is a 16 inch hoop and like the front rim it's chrome plated and surrounded by a Metzeler tire. Though many of the real choppers ran a small drum brake in back and no brake in front, Arlen opted for a disc brake in back and twin discs up front - after all, you can only take this nostalgia thing so far.

The only truly correct engine for an old chopper is a Panhead, and Arlen scrounged enough parts from his personal stash to assemble a nice rebuilt example of the breed. With polished cases and chrome-plated heads, this example probably looks just a shade better than the real McCoy seen under the street lights twenty five years ago.

Where this Panhead breaks company with the real thing of our collective youth is not just in the polishing and chrome plate, but in the details like the air cleaner. While the real thing

Flames, flames, flames, even flames in three dimensions coming from Arlen's unique air cleaner.

would have carried the simple domed air cleaner from Harley-Davidson, Arlen created a flamed air cleaner, with flames in 3-D!

If the Panhead is politically correct for an old chopper, so are the Fat Bob tanks, though these are narrowed a bit and taper gently to the point where they meet the seat. The seat itself is a little solo number stitched up special for the occasion. And surrounding the sixteen inch rear tire is one of Arlen's Tail Dragger fenders,

extended to reach almost all the way to the asphalt.

The wild flames on this old scooter are Arlen's own, laid out in a multi step process that took almost as long as it did to build the bike. Arlen painted the flames himself, starting with the bright orange base paint from the House of

Rear view shows off the 18 inch rim, Metzeler tire, Ness fender and extended and reinforced swingarm.

Looking considerably different from the XR 1000 from which is was created, this Arlen Ness example is longer, lower and much brighter than the original.

ARLEN
NESS

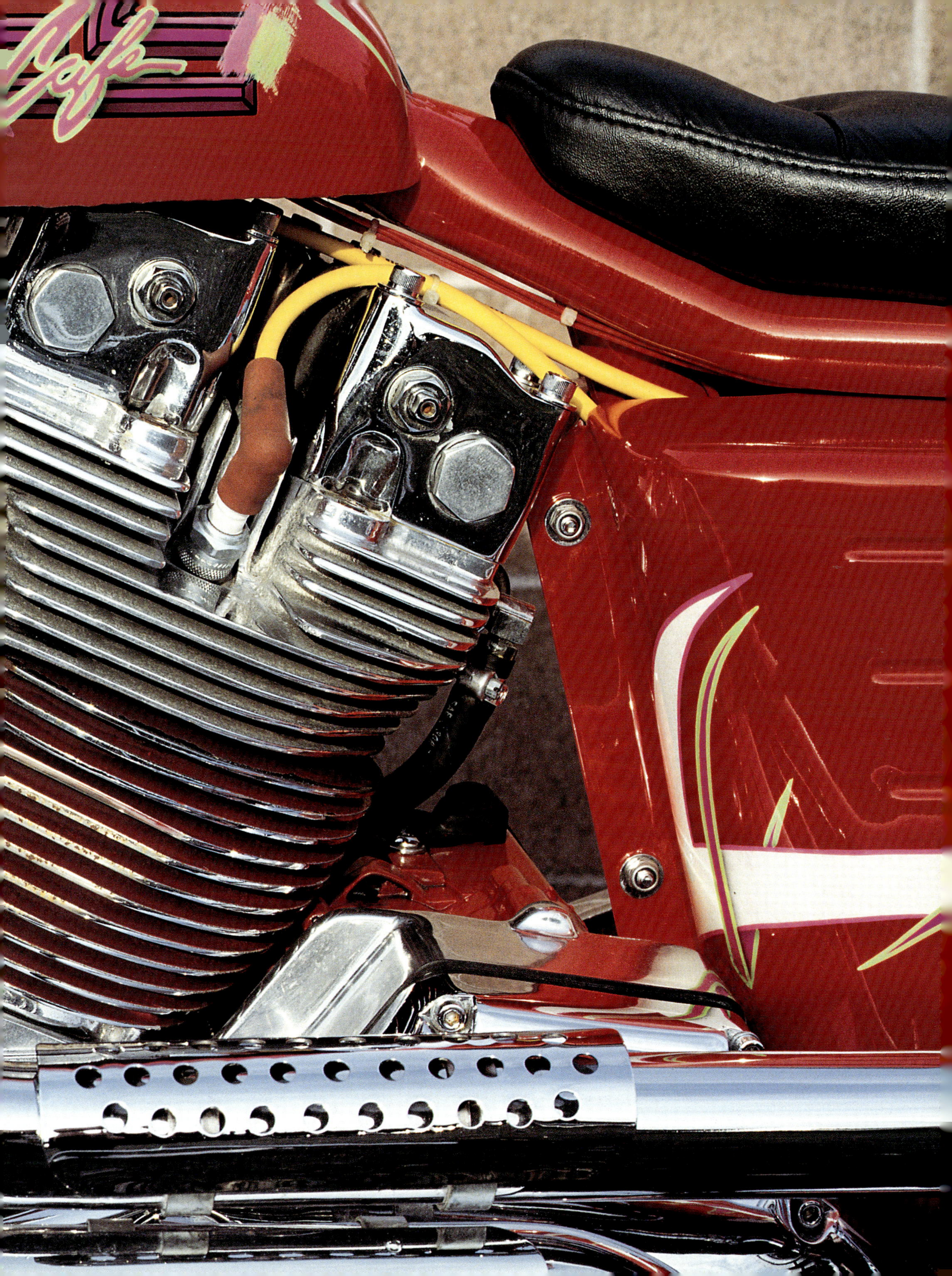

Kolor. Next came the ghost flames hidden under a coat of pearl. Finally Arlen taped off and painted the lime green green flames and had them pinstriped by Ron Morrelli.

Arlen Ness is a hard man to define. Because just when you think you've got him figured, he goes and does something totally different. Just when you're ready to predict that the next bike will surely look like it came off the Enterprise and be powered by a gas turbine, Arlen does a one-eighty and goes retro with the best old

---

The idea was a cafe racer with extra style, added color and minimal trade offs in rideability and purpose. An XR true to its roots yet exhibiting a certain unique-Ness, if you will.

Panhead chopper you've ever seen.

Ness Cafe

Just when it seemed that Arlen was pretty much all done with Sportsters, along comes this new bike called Ness Cafe. Now a Sportster seems an odd duck and an unusual bike for Arlen to build. Except for the fact that he has always like Sportsters, especially those somewhat rare XR 1000 race-based Sportys built by The Motor Company during 1983 and 1984.

Arlen started the project with a less-than-pristine example from the wrecking yard. The idea was a cafe racer with extra style, added color and minimal trade offs in rideability and purpose. An XR true to its roots yet exhibiting a

certain unique-Ness, if you will.

Stock XRs have a stubby, business-like look, and Arlen started the transformation by stretching the bike and getting it closer to the pavement. Arlen increased the fork rake to about 35 degrees and then added three inches to the factory swingarm. While they were modifying the swingarm, Arlen suggested they move the axle mounting point to the top of the swingarm, to reduce the bike's height. To reduce it further, Arlen chose rear shocks one inch shorter than stock and front fork tubes with two inches removed from their length.

XR 1000s share the basic Sportster chassis, complete with the oil tank on the right side and the battery on the left. Arlen wanted side covers, but he didn't want them bulging out around the battery. The solution was the large front air dam, which provided a great place to put the battery. With the battery relocated and the filler for the oil tank moved, it was relatively easy to design and build side covers that wrap around both sides of the motorcycle. The side covers help to lengthen the bike and give it a more finished look.

The twin tanks with the characteristically Sportster profile started life as one large Sportster tank cut in half and thus fashioned into a unique set of Sport-Bob fuel tanks. The fairing is straight from Arlen's catalog, as are the minimalist front and rear "cafe" fenders.

If the styling side of Ness Cafe is much altered, the mechanical aspect is based on factory components with certain improvements. The displacement of the XR mill remains at 1000

By cutting a King Sportster tank in half Arlen and Bob Monroe created their own unique Sport-Bob tanks. Engine is fed by twin Mikuni carbs bolted to one-off manifold with a wedge-shaped air cleaner out front.

ness
cafe

cc, though the performance is enhanced through the use of twin Mikuni carbs bolted to a custom manifold of chrome plated tubing. Visual enhancements to the big mill include polished, plated and painted heads, barrels and cases.

External oil lines have been replaced by Russell braided lines and a wedge shaped air cleaner housing bolts to the carburetors. On the normally boring left side of Ness Cafe we find a pair of hand crafted Bob Monroe pipes and large diameter mufflers, all sparkling in chrome of course.

The spoked wheels measure 18 inches in back and 19 in front. To slow everything down, Arlen chose four-piston calipers from Performance Machine squeezing polished, ven-tilated rotors. The rest of the hardware consists of mostly off-the-shelf parts like the Stealth mirrors and billet grips.

Gleaming in bright red paint with wild graphics, Ness Cafe redefines what a custom Harley-Davidson is, which is pretty much what Arlen's been doing since the days when his Sportsters came with springer forks and diamond gas tanks.

A Basic Black Hot Rod

Arlen's little Hot Rod Bike seems like it might have been built by someone else. Basic and black, this bike hardly looks like one of the extravagant motorcycles that Arlen is best known for. The black Hot Rod Bike displays another side of Arlen Ness. The side that enjoys a straight forward motorcycle. A well-built bike

Another example of what you can do with one of Arlen's five-speed frames - you can build a very sim-ple, clean hot rod with a stroker motor and a very black paint job.

without any frills. A simple, fast motorcycle built to go down the road.

Arlen started with his own, rubber-mount frame and installed a very fast, yet simple, V-twin. The engine uses S&S flywheels to get the displacement to 89 ci. Those cubes are fed by an S&S carb and intake bolted to ported heads with valves operated by a Crane camshaft. Externally, everything was either painted or powder coated in black to match the rest of the bike.

At the front, the little hot rod uses a 19 inch spoked rim, Metzeler tire and dual discs with calipers from Performance Machine. The Streamliner fender is straight from the catalog, set between the shortened narrow-glide fork. Like the front, the rear tire is a Metzler, mounted on an 18 inch alloy rim and spoked wheel assembly. The rear brake is another four-piston caliper from Performance machine, coupled to a polished rotor.

The rear suspension mirrors Arlen's desire to keep everything simple and business-like. The swingarm is a dual-rail design, a special one with the axle mounted on top. The Shock absorbers are premium units from Progressive Suspension will full aluminum bodies for light weight. The rear fender is wide and short, supported by two or Arlen's trick fender struts.

Though most of the bike is built from readily available parts, a few items can only be called custom. Like the hand pounded aluminum gas tanks from Bob Monroe and the small solo seat.

The braided stainless brake lines are used throughout the bike partly because they work and partly because they're part of the performance package. With everything else very simple and black there was only one color Arlen could paint the sheet metal. Arlen used acrylic lacquer from the House of Kolor (the blackest black in the entire world) and then asked ace striper Ron Morrelli to create the nice Harley

The front wheel measures 19 inches while the rear is an 18 inch unit, both use alloy rims mounted with Metzeler tires Brakes are from Performance Machine while the front fender is a catalog item.

logo on the custom gas tanks.

Not fancy or colorful, the little hot rod is the other side of Arlen, the side that simply likes to ride - fast, simple motorcycles.

Chapter Five

The King

Arlen makes it to the top

Life at the top

People who follow custom bikes might wonder at Arlen's growth, might ask: "how much more popular can Arlen get, and how much more can he expect his company to grow?" The answer seems to be that there is no end in sight, either for Arlen's popularity or for the growth of the Arlen Ness parts business.

Builder of the Year, Arlen Ness

Of all the car and motorcycle shows in this great U.S. of A. (home of the the Chrysler 440 Cubic Inch Engine *and* the Harley-Davidson) the Oakland Roadster Show is by far the most prestigious and best known. Anyone who attended the forty-fifth edition of the Grand National Roadster show discovered an enormous display of Arlen Ness motorcycles as soon as they entered the main arena - because Arlen was chosen as Builder of the Year. The man who gave up competing in shows many years earlier was now honored by his peers in both the motorcycle and automotive worlds for consistently creating great designs.

Lest anyone forget the range of Arlen's talents, the bikes on display included three choppers, the full-bodied Ferrari bike, Mona Lisa with its mono-shock suspension and "open" rear fender, the Pro Street Team Ness bike and Arlen's two-bikes-in-one Convertible bike.

The display served as a reminder that Arlen Ness wasn't invited just because he's been building motorcycles for nearly thirty years. He was chosen as Builder of the Year because for almost thirty years Arlen has been producing consistently great motorcycle designs, each one a fresh statement of his talent and drive.

Success brings access to new talent

During a recent conversation with Arlen I asked if it wasn't difficult to consistently come up with fresh ideas and designs, year after year. Arlen explained that in reality it got easier year by year, "For a long time I didn't have much money, so any time I needed something fabricated I had to do it on a swap basis. And I could never just build a bike, I had to sell another bike or re-build an existing bike because there wasn't enough cash to be going out and buying bikes.

It's easier now because I can buy a bike as the start of a new project."

"And I've got access to more parts and tooling. We can make all kinds of new shapes from billet aluminum on CNC equipment, shapes that were almost impossible to build just a few years ago. As for the ideas for the bikes, I still have plenty of new ideas, but now I can hire an artist to fine tune the concept and do a rendering of the bike. It makes it easier to build the bike."

Another of Cory's bikes, this wild purple number is based on an Arlen Ness frame equipped with spoked rims, hand-formed aluminum gas tanks and all the latest billet accessories from the catalog.

All of a sudden, the artists and fabricators are keen to work with me. It's nice to have access to all that talent."

Arlen outgrows another store

In 1988, Arlen, Bev and Cory moved into their third store, with a whopping 5,000 square feet of space. The phenomenal growth of the company means that they were soon giving notice to the tenants in the building next door in their on-going search for more space. With the space next door and some additions the third store has been increased to 15,000 square feet - and there isn't a square foot of those 15,000 that's underutilized. The offices are small and crowded, isles in the warehouse require skinny people to pick orders as more and more floor space yields to shelving.

Arlen has always managed with a conservative hand, always working to minimize company debt. As they outgrow the third location however, the situation requires more than just a bigger store, the continued growth of over forty percent each year demands a quantum leap.

Cory, the man responsible for much of that phenomenal growth, is very much a part of the plans for the new facility. As this book goes to press, Arlen and Cory are finalizing plans for a large store and warehouse facility with enough land to allow for more expansion in the future. The new facility will include a world class retail store and a large, efficient warehouse and shipping facility. The new operation will be nice, it will be large, but it won't be on East Fourteenth street. Rather the new store and warehouse will be inland slightly and right off the freeway for easy access.

Still just a boy at heart

Not everyone can handle success. Stories of Hollywood stars or artists who used to be "regular people" before being discovered are as common as chrome widgets on a Harley. Despite the phenomenal growth of his company, the awards

Seen here with his son Zachary, Cory Ness is now responsible for most day to day decisions as well as long term planning for Arlen Ness, Incorporated.

and the press attention, Arlen Ness remains a quiet, thoughtful and very warm individual.

Motorcycles still intrigue Arlen Ness, the man who still rides to Sturgis each year and still does burn outs outside the bar. Though his face carries a few wrinkles, the eyes still sparkle with excitement at a new idea or a particularly sexy motorcycle.

What Arlen Ness does best is design and build motorcycles and motorcycle parts. If there's a part of the recent expansion and success that he doesn't particularly care for, it's the constant attention the business requires. Negotiating prices, discussions with bankers, worries about the best computer system, this is not the kind of thing that Arlen enjoys.

Five years ago, Cory's increasing involve-

Arlen and Bev Ness, the young couple who rented the first store for $100 per month, now leave more and more of the business in the hands of Cory Ness.

ment was supposed to give Arlen more time in his small sanctuary - the shop at home. Business is business however, and it required that Arlen stay very "hands on" at the store. Decisions worth thousands and thousand of dollars are made daily, and many of those require Arlen's input.

Is there no way out?

Arlen's success has brought a variety of offers from investors, all of whom have an idea how Arlen Ness might make better use of his talent and name recognition. One idea that keeps resurfacing is the notion of building "Arlen Ness" motorcycles. Based on an aftermarket V-twin engine and transmission combined with an Arlen Ness frame, these bikes would provide a means for Arlen to focus on building new motorcycles.

After thirty years in the motorcycle business, Arlen Ness has no plans for retirement. During a recent conversation in Sturgis Arlen explained that what people think he should do and what he wants to do are two very different things. "People think I should retire because now I'm successful. What they forget is that this is fun. I get to design motorcycles and motorcycle parts. When we go on a business trip, I'm always meeting these interesting people and they want to meet me. We ride and have dinner and talk about new ideas. I might want to cut back my hours a little as the years go by, but I like what I do. What would I do if I retired, go sit some-place where there aren't any motorcycles?"

What the future holds for Arlen Ness is less involvement in the day to day business of selling accessories and more opportunities to design and build killer custom bikes. Anyone who wonders if Arlen might someday run out of ideas need only look as far as the bikes on the floor of the store. There's Two Bad, the Ferrari bike, the Convertible, Mona Lisa, the list goes on and on. Each bike is a bold statement and a radical departure from other bikes built during the same period. For Arlen Ness there is no shortage of ideas, only a shortage of time to implement those ideas.

Arlen Ness speaks not of retiring, but of new opportunities to build motorcycles. A chance to design bikes no one has even thought of yet. After thirty years, he isn't slowing down, but accelerating. With more time Arlen can design more bikes - wild new bikes that could only come from one man - the kid from San Leandro. The one who started with that little Cushman scooter — a guy named Arlen Ness.

THE MOTORCYCLES

A Bright New Luxury Liner

It all started with a stretched black FXRT that came to be known as the Bat Bike. Not the best known of Arlen's many designs, the Bat Bike might have been just a flash in the pan, except for Arlen's ability to recognize a great idea and stick with it.

The Bat Bike started life as an FXRT, or the touring version of the then-current rubber-mount chassis. The advantages of this package included the rubber mounted engine for a vibration free ride, belt drive and a wealth of accessories available to fit the bike. The touring package included a large fairing, bags and a tour pak.

The FXRT made a great rider, though most riders considered the bike to be the ugly duckling of the Harley-Davidson family. Arlen's job then was to improve the looks and keep the bike a very functional ride.

The Bat Bike was the first in a series of

This Yellow Screamer is one of a series of Luxury Liners, so named because of their comfort and style.

FXRTs, the first rung in a long evolutionary ladder. With its modified fairing, lowered seat height and long tail dragger fenders, the Bat Bike took on some style missing from the stock bike and left the best parts of the FXRT experience intact.

The current apogee of that ladder, the conclusion of a great idea if you will, is the Screaming Yellow Zonker. The most current of the bikes that have come to be called Luxury Liners.

The Yellow Screamer is long and low, the result of some serious chassis modifications. Arlen stretched the chassis three inches and then

kicked the front wheel out to a total rake of about thirty six degrees. By cutting the fork tubes and installing shorter rear shocks, the bike came down much closer to terra firma. And if that's not low enough, Arlen cut the frame tubes under the seat and lowered the seat so the rider's fanny would ride one inch closer to the pavement.

The fairing benefits from a weight loss plan that includes the removal of material along the bottom edge and on the inside. The sides of the fairing have been pulled in, giving it a more streamlined shape. Though most of the earlier bikes have come equipped with large leather bags, the yellow bike features one-off hard bags built by Bob Monroe from sheet aluminum.

And like the earlier bikes, this yellow monster is equipped with tail dragger fenders, extended at the bottom lip to drag even closer to the ground.

Power for the yellow bike is an 80 ci V-twin equipped with a Crane cam, mild headwork and a S&S Series E carburetor. Though the insides remain largely stock, the outside is definitely dressed for success in the latest billet accessories.

Rockerboxes, air cleaner, push rod tubes, lifter blocks and cam cover are all carved from solid chunks of aluminum - the latest in Arlen's new line of billet engine accessories. The heads and barrels are painted to match the bike while the engine cases are polished. The transmission too carries billet covers and throws light off the sparkling polished case. Bub pipes, very popular of late, provide an exit route for all that spent gas.

The Luxury liners are built for comfort, built to cruise at high speed all day long. In fact, the yellow bike is the one Arlen rode to Sturgis, the one that never so much as hiccuped on the trip. Arlen reports that the bike is comfortable and easy to ride. The international sprockets provide a higher gear ratio for lazy highway cruising, the low seating position means that the bike kind of wraps around the rider providing a great spot from which to pilot the motorcycle.

Built for comfort and for speed, the latest luxury liner shows what happens when you take a good idea and make it better and better.

Team Ness

Arlen Ness is a man who enjoys fast motorcycles. Drag race motorcycles in particular hold a certain fascination for Arlen. In fact, the

This FXR is powered by an 80 ci Evo equipped with all the latest billet accessories from Arlen and Cory, including their billet air cleaner, push rod tubes and lifter blocks.

ARLEN
NESS

styling cues from those go-fast two wheelers sometimes find their way into certain of Arlen's designs. Witness Arlen's early non-choppers with their Lowliner frames and stretched profiles. Now fast forward to the present and examine another unique Arlen Ness design. One based on some very sleek body work, a long chin spoiler, a fat, low profile rear tire and a true hot rod motor.

Team Ness borrows again from styling cues seen more commonly at the drag strip in the guise of a Pro Street bike. The rear fender is round and large enough to cover a big hairy rear tire. Up front, there's the small fairing with a bulge just big enough for the all-important tachometer. Below that there's a long narrow air dam to help keep the front wheel on the track. The lines are much different than those seen on street bikes, be they dressers or cafe bikes. This is another bike that breaks away from the pack with a whole series of unique styling ideas.

Arlen started the project, as he often does,

Team Ness borrows the Pro Street look with flowing aluminum panels formed by Bob Monroe.

Underneath it's an Arlen Ness five-speed frame and hot rod V-twin with four-valve heads.

with the construction of a rolling chassis. The chassis then would determine the basic dimensions for the extensive body work to follow.

Once he knew the dimensions for the bike, Arlen hired a young artist, Carl Brouhard, to do a rendering of the bike. With a rolling chassis and a set of thorough sketches, Arlen could turn to Bob Monroe for the fabrication of the rounded body panels that would define this new motorcycle.

Bob formed the panels from sheet aluminum, working from Carl's sketches with input from Arlen. First the rear fender and side panels, then the small fairing. The gas tanks too are hand formed aluminum, as is the long front air dam. The front fender was easier, and involved only the modification of a stock Arlen Ness catalog fender.

The rolling chassis that Arlen constructed is based on his own five-speed rubber-mount

Note the unusual left side - with both a carburetor and an exhaust pipe. Black paint is Arlen's with race-team graphics by Carl Brouhard.

Team
Ness
CAL
DLR 5A 20382

frame. For motive power Arlen wanted more than just a mildly leaned on stock Evo engine. The foundation for this hot rod motor is a set of Sputhe Nitralloy polished cases mated to stroker flywheels from S&S. The "big wheels" and stock diameter barrels and pistons yield an 89 ci V-twin, and a good start on a full-tilt-boogie motor.

Engineers say that an internal combustion engine is really just an air pump - that the more air an engine pumps the more power it makes. In the case of Arlen's new engine, the air enters through two (yes, one on each side) S&S series E carburetors, before passing through the intake side of the four-valve Fueling-Rivera heads and finally out via the multiple exhaust valves and the custom fabricated -and VERY LOUD - Bob Monroe pipes. A high lift Crane cam ensures that all those valves go up far enough and stay there long enough to ensure that plenty of gas and air enter and exit each cylinder.

Most people would have used a pair of S&S air cleaners for the twin carbs, but then you need to remember, this is Team Ness. Each carb hides under a billet air cleaner, and both sides of the engine are covered in billet cam and derby covers. The transmission glitters with that same shine, the result of the polished cases and billet end covers. Even the master cylinder and lever for the rear wheel are carved from that light-weight material.

All those horses travel through a primary chain to the relocated transmission. In order to run the fat 180x18 inch rear tire and have the

Left side of Arlen's big V-twin shows the extra carbu-retor used to feed the four-valve heads. Engine displaces 89 ci with help from an S&S stroker bottom end.

chain sprockets line up, Arlen had to move the transmission over to the left. The large Metzeler mounts on a spoked rim measuring 5-3/4 inches in width. A narrow front rim mounts another Metzeler tire, this one 19 inches in diameter.

Hot rods need good brakes, so they can slow as well as they go. The front brakes do most of the work of course, thus Arlen bolted two

Performance Machine four-piston calipers to the lower fork legs and a pair of polished rotors to the front hub. The rear brakes use another pol-

Small fairing is contoured to accept the all-important tachometer - with no speedometer in sight. Like any good race bike, this one uses caps vented to a small catch-can set in the fairing.

Rear fender has a rounded shape and enough room to cover the fat 18 inch Metzeler tire. Rear brakes use a single caliper from Performance Machine.

OKLAHOMA
GEORGES.
KILLER
KLEIN

ished rotor spinning between the jaws of another caliper from Performance Machine.

The colors for the Team Ness bike are the result of a collaboration between Arlen and Carl, the artist and painter. Arlen applied the black while Carl did the orange and white stripes and Arlen's logo.

Team Ness is a completely new motorcycle. Not a chopper and not really a futuristic bike, but instead a brand new type of custom created by combining Pro Street looks in a street bike chassis.

The very tall ape-hanger bars bolt directly to the springer fork legs. Note the wild upswept pipes and unusual wrap around oil tank.

This is one sexy Sportster tank, massaged by Bob Monroe to wrap close to the Shovel-heads. Engine is a dressed out example of the last pre-Evo, with an S&S carburetor and a billet air cleaner from Arlen.

One more chopper

Less comfortable, though perhaps more pure fun than the Yellow Screamer, the Shovelhead chopper is part of a matched set of choppers and close kin to the Panhead chopper seen elsewhere in this book.

For some people, one chopper would be enough, but Arlen explains that, "The choppers are fun to build and fun to run around on. They remind me of the days when I was just getting started."

In those days of yesteryear the choppers were built along conservative lines, thus this Shovel combines a hardtail frame with a short springer fork from Paughco. Longer than the fork are the reach-for-the-sky bars equipped with a pair of very modern billet grips and mirror.

The motor for this particular chopper is a Shovelhead, the last of the pre-Evolution engines. This particular Shovelhead has been improved considerably in terms of both looks and performance. Outside, the heads and barrels shine brighter than new, due to the chrome plated fins and bright red paint. Billet push rod tubes, air cleaner and various covers help to remind the careful viewer that this isn't really 1965. Internally the engine is near stock, rebuilt and improved with the addition of a Crane cam and pushrods, and a Series E carburetor from S&S.

Sportster tanks were popular on the original choppers, and this retro ride is equipped with a king Sportster tank, massaged considerably by Bob Monroe to better fit the frame and arch

The Sled shown in fully dressed condition. Seen this way, it's hard to believe that there's another complete *motorcycle under all that body work.*

gracefully over this Shovel's heads. Behind the gas tank is an unusual oil bag, with tapered tails that extend all the way back to the rear axle. The final piece of sheet metal isn't metal at all. The fiberglass rear fender has been both widened and extended, and rides on small, arched fender supports. At the very bottom is nice touch, the chrome plated trim along the edge.

A wide 180x18 inch Metzeler tire mounted to a spoked rim resides under the fat fender, chain driven from the transmission. Up front another Metzeler 21 inch tire surrounds a trim spoked rim.

The paint job on the Shovelhead is similar to the Panhead, only the base color here is red, with subtle ghost flames and finally some very bright flames in yellow and red.

In the end the chopper is a simple bike. Built to follow an old style, built to be simple, bright and more than anything else - fun.

The Roadster, or convertible side of The Sled, complete with minimalist tank and bobbed fenders.

Mona Lisa, part of the Concept Collection

It must be a wonderful thing, to have as many great design ideas rattling around in your head as Arlen Ness does. To be able to go from designing and building the race-bred Team Ness to the ultra long and lean Mona Lisa. All of it

Mona Lisa carries some very nice body work including this front fender that wraps close to the disc brake rotor and runs parallel to the frame along the back side.

done in a short period of time and all while running a business and working on other projects at the same time.

Mona Lisa goes in a totally different direction than other contemporary Arlen Ness bikes and does so with a new chassis and some very fresh sheet metal. Because the bike breaks with past tradition and introduces a whole series of new parts and new styling concepts, Arlen is making it part of his Concept Collection. The Concept Collection is a one of Arlen's new ideas,

Mona Lisa's most unusual feature is this "open" rear fender - just one more innovation from the man

who's been giving us what we didn't always know we liked for almost 30 years.

made up of bikes that make major departures from current trends and help point the way for the future.

When Arlen started on Mona Lisa, he wanted it long and low. No, that should read, very long and very low. "We stretched the frame and then we stretched the swingarm," explains Arlen, "and then we added things like the extra long floor boards and long narrow air cleaner to make it seem even longer than it really is."

The chassis is a rubber mount design,

The engine is a near stock Evo displacing 80 ci. Note the air cleaner, gas tanks and chrome strips on *the front fender, all part of this very long creation.*

ARLEN NESS

The man with the twinkle in his eye is Arlen Ness - older and wiser but still excited about motorcycles. Especially all those bikes rolling around in his head just waiting to be built.

floating rotors from Performance Machine - special rotors with Arlen's logo machined into the surface - with the latest six piston aluminum calipers from Billet 6.

Wrapped close to the rotors is the aluminum front fender crafted by Bob Monroe, shaped so the backside of the fender angles down at the same angle as the frame tubes. The gas tanks definitely aren't Fat Bobs. Designed to be long and skinny, the tanks fit the theme of the bike and stretch w-a-a-a-y back until they meet the seat. Under the seat are the side covers, flared slightly and cut to wrap around the primary cover on one side and the transmission on the other, the side covers help make the design flow and also hide the shock absorber and its linkage.

The other really unique part of this bike is

With a new chassis and some very unusual body work, Mona Lisa is the latest - though certainly not the last - great design to come from the mind of Arlen Ness.

---

stretched five inches. To keep the bike very narrow, Arlen chose to eliminate the shock absorbers from the side of the bike. The stretched swingarm is connected to a single shock absorber mounted between the transmission and rear wheel through linkage similar to that used on modern dirt bikes. The monoshock frame gave rise to the Mona (or mono) Lisa name.

More than the frame of Mona Lisa is new. Up front the lower fork tubes have been polished smooth and contain no provision for bolting on the axle. The axle is held in place by a sleeved clamp assembly on each side that can be slid up and down the tubes for easy height adjustments. The brakes combine enormous

the rear fender. Formed again from aluminum by Bob Monroe, the fender is cut off at the back side and left completely open, to better show off the 180x18 inch Metzeler tire.

The engine for Mona Lisa is a mild 80 ci V-twin with just a few improvements, like the S&S carb, Crane cam and extra long straight pipes with anti reversion cones. The billet air cleaner is a one-off piece, designed to help stretch the bike's profile. The ribs milled into the air cleaner match the ribs in the standard Arlen Ness cam, transmission and derby covers.

There are a few more things that really help this extra long design to come together. The small chrome ribs on the fenders for example started as strips of brass stock formed by Bob Monroe and then sent out for chrome plating. And the billet aluminum floor boards with rubber cushions, much longer than anything available through the catalog.

Finished in black with contrasting chrome strips, Arlen's Mono shock design takes on a very elegant look. Almost like someone took a long beautiful Duesenberg and cut a section - a very thin section - out to leave it standing on two wheels instead of four.

A good bike for the new Concept Collection, Mona Lisa is also a good reminder that Arlen never suffers from a shortage of ideas. With a new chassis and some very unusual body work, Mona Lisa is the latest - though certainly not the last - great design to come from the mind of Arlen Ness.

The next big project is this two-wheeled '57 Chevy - guaranteed to be another giant people-pleaser from the King of the Customizers, Arlen Ness.